TRANSIT COOPERATIVE RESEARCH PROGRAM

Report 51

A Guidebook for Marketing Transit Services to Business

MULTISYSTEMS, INC.
Cambridge, MA
with
ORAM ASSOCIATES, INC.
Englewood, NJ
and
CLAIRE BARRETT & ASSOCIATES
Cambridge, MA

Subject Areas

Public Transit

Research Sponsored by the Federal Transit Administration in Cooperation with the Transit Development Corporation

TRANSPORTATION RESEARCH BOARD
NATIONAL RESEARCH COUNCIL

NATIONAL ACADEMY PRESS
Washington, D.C. 1999

TRANSIT COOPERATIVE RESEARCH PROGRAM

The nation's growth and the need to meet mobility, environmental, and energy objectives place demands on public transit systems. Current systems, some of which are old and in need of upgrading, must expand service area, increase service frequency, and improve efficiency to serve these demands. Research is necessary to solve operating problems, to adapt appropriate new technologies from other industries, and to introduce innovations into the transit industry. The Transit Cooperative Research Program (TCRP) serves as one of the principal means by which the transit industry can develop innovative near-term solutions to meet demands placed on it.

The need for TCRP was originally identified in *TRB Special Report 213—Research for Public Transit: New Directions*, published in 1987 and based on a study sponsored by the Urban Mass Transportation Administration—now the Federal Transit Administration (FTA). A report by the American Public Transit Association (APTA), *Transportation 2000*, also recognized the need for local, problem-solving research. TCRP, modeled after the longstanding and successful National Cooperative Highway Research Program, undertakes research and other technical activities in response to the needs of transit service providers. The scope of TCRP includes a variety of transit research fields including planning, service configuration, equipment, facilities, operations, human resources, maintenance, policy, and administrative practices.

TCRP was established under FTA sponsorship in July 1992. Proposed by the U.S. Department of Transportation, TCRP was authorized as part of the Intermodal Surface Transportation Efficiency Act of 1991 (ISTEA). On May 13, 1992, a memorandum agreement outlining TCRP operating procedures was executed by the three cooperating organizations: FTA, the National Academy of Sciences, acting through the Transportation Research Board (TRB); and the Transit Development Corporation, Inc. (TDC), a nonprofit educational and research organization established by APTA. TDC is responsible for forming the independent governing board, designated as the TCRP Oversight and Project Selection (TOPS) Committee.

Research problem statements for TCRP are solicited periodically but may be submitted to TRB by anyone at any time. It is the responsibility of the TOPS Committee to formulate the research program by identifying the highest priority projects. As part of the evaluation, the TOPS Committee defines funding levels and expected products.

Once selected, each project is assigned to an expert panel, appointed by the Transportation Research Board. The panels prepare project statements (requests for proposals), select contractors, and provide technical guidance and counsel throughout the life of the project. The process for developing research problem statements and selecting research agencies has been used by TRB in managing cooperative research programs since 1962. As in other TRB activities, TCRP project panels serve voluntarily without compensation.

Because research cannot have the desired impact if products fail to reach the intended audience, special emphasis is placed on disseminating TCRP results to the intended end users of the research: transit agencies, service providers, and suppliers. TRB provides a series of research reports, syntheses of transit practice, and other supporting material developed by TCRP research. APTA will arrange for workshops, training aids, field visits, and other activities to ensure that results are implemented by urban and rural transit industry practitioners.

The TCRP provides a forum where transit agencies can cooperatively address common operational problems. The TCRP results support and complement other ongoing transit research and training programs.

TCRP REPORT 51

Project B-8 FY'95
ISSN 1073-4872
ISBN 0-309-06603-4
Library of Congress Catalog Card No. 99-71034

© 1999 Transportation Research Board

Price $22.00

NOTICE

The project that is the subject of this report was a part of the Transit Cooperative Research Program conducted by the Transportation Research Board with the approval of the Governing Board of the National Research Council. Such approval reflects the Governing Board's judgment that the project concerned is appropriate with respect to both the purposes and resources of the National Research Council.

The members of the technical advisory panel selected to monitor this project and to review this report were chosen for recognized scholarly competence and with due consideration for the balance of disciplines appropriate to the project. The opinions and conclusions expressed or implied are those of the research agency that performed the research, and while they have been accepted as appropriate by the technical panel, they are not necessarily those of the Transportation Research Board, the National Research Council, the Transit Development Corporation, or the Federal Transit Administration of the U.S. Department of Transportation.

Each report is reviewed and accepted for publication by the technical panel according to procedures established and monitored by the Transportation Research Board Executive Committee and the Governing Board of the National Research Council.

To save time and money in disseminating the research findings, the report is essentially the original text as submitted by the research agency. This report has not been edited by TRB.

Special Notice

The Transportation Research Board, the National Research Council, the Transit Development Corporation, and the Federal Transit Administration (sponsor of the Transit Cooperative Research Program) do not endorse products or manufacturers. Trade or manufacturers' names appear herein solely because they are considered essential to the clarity and completeness of the project reporting.

Published reports of the

TRANSIT COOPERATIVE RESEARCH PROGRAM

are available from:

Transportation Research Board
National Research Council
2101 Constitution Avenue, N.W.
Washington, D.C. 20418

and can be ordered through the Internet at
http://www.nas.edu/trb/index.html

Printed in the United States of America

FOREWORD

*By Staff
Transportation Research
Board*

TCRP Report 51, "A Guidebook for Marketing Transit Services to Business" provides information on successful business-to-business marketing techniques with application to transit. The Guidebook provides motivation for doing business-to-business marketing, lessons from the private sector as well as the transit industry, guidance on how to implement a business-to-business marketing program, tools and techniques for business-to-business marketing, and evaluation measures. The report should be useful to transit planners, managers, marketing professionals, and others interested in the use of marketing strategies to build ridership.

Traditionally, public transportation agencies have marketed directly to riders and potential riders. In recent years, many transit agencies and regional planning agencies have directed more of their marketing efforts toward business as one means of counteracting declining market share. Employer subsidy programs, guaranteed ride home programs, and nontraditional or customized transit services have been outgrowths of these efforts. Nonetheless, the transit industry, in general, has less experience in business-to-business marketing than do for-profit industries whose entire livelihood often depends on successfully targeting business customers. There is a substantial body of private-sector knowledge of the business-to-business marketing process, business-to-business marketing techniques, and marketing-oriented management that is transferable to the public sector. Thus, there is a need to identify the most effective and broadly applicable business-to-business marketing techniques that public transportation agencies can use.

Multisystems, Inc., in association with Oram Associates, Inc. and Claire Barrett & Associates, was the contractor for TCRP Project B-8 and prepared the guidebook and the final report. To achieve the project objectives of identifying business-to-business marketing methods appropriate for use in the public transit industry and developing a guidebook that can be used by transit professionals for product development and business development, the researchers conducted a comprehensive review of the literature on current marketing practices to identify successful business-to-business marketing methods potentially applicable to transit. Further, criteria were developed to evaluate practices and methods used in business-to-business marketing and transit-to-business marketing. Four in-depth case studies were performed that demonstrate techniques and strategies that can be applied to a broad range of transit agencies. The analysis in each case study includes the background, situation analysis, methods of marketing used, customer-buying styles, and the reasons why these methods are applicable to transit.

A summary of the lessons from business-to-business marketing, emphasizing the key elements of sales and institutional change is also included. Finally, an approach for developing and implementing a transit-to-business marketing plan was completed.

The final report, the companion piece to this guidebook, is titled "Marketing Transit Services to Business." It can be found on the TCRP home page (www4.nas.edu/trb/crp.nsf) on the Internet's World Wide Web as TCRP Web Document 8. The report provides a comprehensive review of business-to-business marketing theory. The final report summarizes the differences between business-to-business and business-to-consumer marketing, and the resulting implications for transit-to-business programs. Also, the final report reviews the marketing process behind most successful programs and highlights tools and techniques that have been proven effective in business-to-business marketing. The final report concludes with a summary on "lessons learned" from the research effort.

CONTENTS

1-1 CHAPTER 1 Overview
Introduction, 1-1
The Benefits Are Mutual, 1-1
The Challenges, 1-6
How To Use This Report, 1-7

2-1 CHAPTER 2 Lessons from the Marketplace
Overview, 2-1
Product Development, 2-1
Effective Sales Techniques, 2-2

3-1 CHAPTER 3 Getting Started
Overview, 3-1
Set Goals, 3-1
Define the Market, 3-2
Develop the Product, 3-6

4-1 CHAPTER 4 Tools and Techniques
Overview, 4-1
Direct Sales, 4-5
Rider-Based Marketing, 4-6
Personal Selling, 4-7
Partnerships, 4-11
Advertising and Publicity, 4-13

5-1 CHAPTER 5 Refinement and Reinforcement
Overview, 5-1
Measures of Effectiveness, 5-1
Customer Satisfaction, 5-3
Feedback, 5-3

6-1 CHAPTER 6 Conclusions
Requirements for Success, 6-3
Transit-to-Business Marketing Tools, 6-3
Program Evaluation, 6-4
Future Opportunities, 6-4

COOPERATIVE RESEARCH PROGRAMS STAFF

ROBERT J. REILLY, *Director, Cooperative Research Programs*
STEPHEN J. ANDRLE, *Manager, Transit Cooperative Research Program*
GWEN CHISHOLM, *Senior Program Officer*
EILEEN P. DELANEY, *Managing Editor*
NATASSJA K. LINZAU, *Senior Editorial Assistant*

PROJECT PANEL B-8

KAY VAN SICKEL, *Oregon DOT* (Chair)
CARMINO N. BASILE, *Capital District Transportation Authority, Albany, NY*
JANICE L. BLAHUT, *Port Authority of Allegheny County, Pittsburgh, PA*
DEBORAH A. COOPER, *Port Authority of Allegheny County, Pittsburgh, PA*
RONALD L. FREELAND, *Maryland Mass Transit Administration*
SAMUEL SEWARD, *Milwaukee County Transit System*
LORRAINE K. TAYLOR, *Washington Metropolitan Area Transit Authority, Washington, DC*
ROBERT VITALE, *San Jose, CA*
WILLIAM MENCZER, *FTA Liaison Representative*
ROBERT WASHINGTON, *FTA Liaison Representative*
PETER SHAW, *TRB Liaison Representative*

AUTHOR ACKNOWLEDGMENTS

The research reported herein was performed under TCRP Project B-8 by Multisystems, Inc., Oram Asociates, Inc., and Claire Barrett & Associates. Multisystems was the contractor for the study, whereas the work performed by Oram Associates and Claire Barrett & Associates was under a subcontract with Multisystems, Inc.

Karla Karash, Vice President of Multisystems, Inc., was the principal investigator, with overall responsibility for the project. Susan Bregman of Multisystems and Richard Oram of Oram Associates were the principal authors of the Guidebook. Helpful input was provided by Claire Barrett of Claire Barrett & Associates.

Background case studies were conducted by Raisa Lawrence, Susan Bregman, and Richard Oram. The production contribution of Kevin Newton of Multisystems is also appreciated.

Multisystems appreciates the assistance and cooperation of the managers at Pace, Bank of America, Kaiser Permanente, the various voucher programs, and other transit and ridesharing agencies for providing the examples used throughout the Guidebook. The guidance of the B-8 project panel and of Gwen Chisholm of TCRP is also gratefully acknowledged.

Chapter 1

Overview

Introduction

Traditionally, public transportation agencies have marketed their services directly to riders and potential riders. In response to changing market conditions, however, a number of transit agencies have begun to direct more of their marketing efforts toward businesses whose employees and customers are potential users. Many transit agencies have worked closely with employers, in particular, to promote a range of services, including ridesharing, prepaid pass and voucher programs, guaranteed rides home, and customized services. Still others have worked with local planning bodies or private developers to incorporate transit-friendly elements into site design, while others have worked with local retailers and institutions on joint marketing efforts. Table 1-1 describes the full range of transit-to-business marketing activities.

Although private sector businesses have extensive experience in business-to-business marketing, transit agencies may not be familiar with the specific techniques associated with marketing their services directly to the business community. Accordingly, this workbook is designed to provide transit agencies with the hands-on information needed to undertake successful transit-to-business marketing programs. Examples are drawn from two sources. First, the book presents lessons from the business community designed to guide transit operators on the process of marketing their services to businesses. Second, it provides a practical compendium of successful transit marketing techniques for operators to adapt to their own systems.

The Benefits Are Mutual

Transit providers and the business community are natural partners. Working with the business community can help transit operators gain ridership, expand revenues, and generate broad-based community support. Businesses, in turn, can stay competitive while improving their public image – and save money at the same time.

Advantages to Transit

The benefits to transit of working with the business community are substantial. Although businesses do not consume transit directly, their employees, customers, and clients do. Rather than attempting to reach individual riders, which is difficult without extensive advertising and promotional budgets, marketing to employers – along with universities, shopping malls, and other activity centers – allows a transit property to reach many potential riders through a single targeted approach. This approach is analogous to wholesale marketing, where the employer takes the place of the wholesaler. Advantages to this approach include the following.

- **Ridership and revenue.** Marketing directly to business, particularly employers, can attract new transit riders and generate additional revenues.

- **Cost-effectiveness.** By marketing directly to businesses, transit agencies can reach a concentrated group of current and potential customers in an efficient and cost effective way.

- **Targeted message.** Because employees, students, or other business customers often have similar travel patterns, transit agencies can target their marketing message and services.

- **Community support.** By working closely with the business community, transit operators have an opportunity to gain visibility and to develop allies for current and future programs.

This relationship allows transit agencies to increase the efficiency of their marketing programs. Instead of the traditional approach, which aims generalized advertising and marketing programs at individual passengers, marketing directly to business enables transit agencies to target their message and reach numerous potential consumers at once. In effect, the business community provides an efficient distribution network for transit to identify and communicate with current and potential riders.

Benefits for Business

What about the business community? Working with transit agencies to improve access to sites can save money, improve productivity, and benefit businesses in a number of other ways.

- **Save money.** For employers in densely developed cities, parking may be prohibitively expensive to provide. Not only can promoting ridesharing or subsidizing transit fares save employers the cost of expensive parking, but such benefits can be provided tax free to employees and considered a business expense by employers.

- **Improve access.** Businesses can work with transit agencies to improve access to their facilities in a number of ways – by promoting use of existing transit services and by developing new services (such as reverse commute service, suburban shuttles, or guaranteed ride home programs). Improved access can help businesses recruit and retain employees and serve their clients more effectively.

- **Improve competitiveness.** Transit or ridesharing has been shown to reduce employee stress, improve morale, and otherwise improve perceptions of the workplace. This in turn can increase productivity, reduce employee turnover, and—again—save the employer money.

- **Reduce congestion.** Encouraging increased use of public transit can help reduce congestion and air pollution. Moreover, federal, state, and local regulations have required many employers or developers to encourage employees to use mass transit, especially in larger cities or congested suburbs.

Ultimately, transit programs are one more way for businesses to gain a competitive edge within their field. The advantages may be direct and quantifiable; offering transit benefits, for example, may increase the value of

---

It's official: Commuting causes stress

A state-financed study in Southern California found commuting stress significantly related to distance and duration of one's commute. Highest stress was reported by women commuting 20 miles or more; 48 percent of female solo drivers in long-distance commutes who reported that exposure to traffic congestion has negative impacts on their family life also said they would like to try carpooling.

Table 1-1
Examples of Major Transit-to-Business Marketing Actions

Action	Description
On-site pass sales	Passes sold at work site
Pass subsidies	Subsidized passes sold at work site
University Pass / EcoPass Programs	Annual pass for all students/employees sold at major discounts
Vouchers	Scrip sold to employers for employees to use when buying tickets or passes
Credit card / Third-party billing	Employer is billed for employees' rides
Carpooling	Shared ride matching services; promotional support
Vanpooling	Shared ride for longer distance users; leasing plans
Guaranteed ride home	Provides ride home in emergencies for employees using transit or ridesharing.
Employee transportation coordinators	Staff provided by employer/developer to promote transit, ridesharing, and other transportation demand management strategies
Transportation management associations	Employers/developers who jointly adopt traffic reduction activities
Shuttle services	Local connectors to regional transit or activity centers
Circulator services	Internal circulation at large sites
Subscription services	Develop special bus route for certain destinations
Reverse commute services	Connections for city residents to access suburban employment sites
Modifying existing services	Matching schedules or route to special needs
Transit enhancements/amenities	Access improvements, including shelters and walkways
Site design initiatives	Building modifications to support transit access
Employer survey assistance	Identifying employee transportation needs
Relocation services	Assisting new employers/developments
New employee orientation materials	Provide new employees with information about transportation alternatives
Transit information services	Inform employers about transit services and emergency situations
Retail incentives	Partnerships with retailers to promote transit use
Regulatory initiatives	Regulations governing land use, density, parking, transportation demand management

The Benefits of Transit-to-Business Marketing

Many transit-business marketing programs have long- term or intangible benefits, but the following show that very tangible short-term results also arise.

Voucher Programs: Inducing a key downtown employer to subsidize employee transit fares to offset higher parking prices, the Milwaukee County Transit System (MCTS) increased transit riding at one site by 81 percent, adding over $90,000 a year in MCTS revenue from a single employer. Similarly, among 150 employers in the San Francisco Bay Area that had recently begun subsidizing fares, transit use rose by an average of over 31 percent. Over 7,000 employers have bought TransitCheks in Greater New York, for annual fare subsidies exceeding $50 million.

Employer Pass Plans: Fare subsidies have actually become a standard in some cities. For example, in Seattle and Des Moines, more than half the passes sold are employer-subsidized. In Boston, MBTA's Pass Program serves over 1,000 employers. Denver's ECOPASS all-employee subsidy program provides free transit passes to over 50,000 users, with fares paid by their employers.

Promotional Subsidies: For Try Transit Week in 1997, Houston Metro offered weekly passes for employers to purchase for their entire staff at $1 per employee. The promotion yielded 60,000 more boardings than a similar promotion in 1996.

Guaranteed Ride Home : Employers willingly embrace these programs, which provide a high level of assurance to employees who rideshare or use transit that they will be able to get home in emergencies. The guaranteed ride home program is an examples of a service that matches a significant business concern, can be simple to administer, and has a low cost but high perceived benefits. In a Minnesota survey, 58 percent of employees enrolled in guaranteed ride home programs reported it either very or somewhat important to their decision to use the bus, car/vanpool or bike to work.

Marketing Transit Services to Business

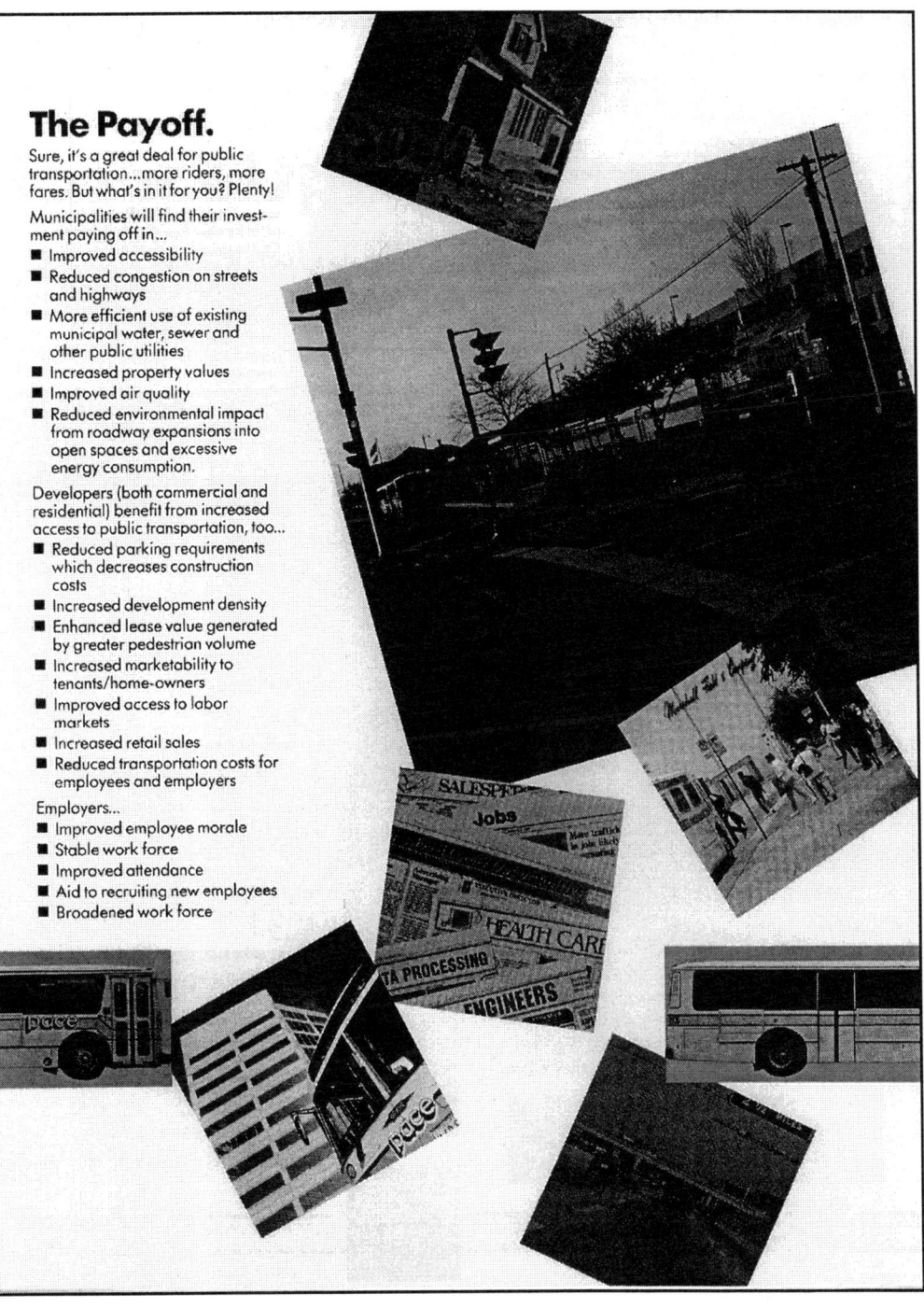

The Payoff.

Sure, it's a great deal for public transportation...more riders, more fares. But what's in it for you? Plenty!

Municipalities will find their investment paying off in...
- Improved accessibility
- Reduced congestion on streets and highways
- More efficient use of existing municipal water, sewer and other public utilities
- Increased property values
- Improved air quality
- Reduced environmental impact from roadway expansions into open spaces and excessive energy consumption.

Developers (both commercial and residential) benefit from increased access to public transportation, too...
- Reduced parking requirements which decreases construction costs
- Increased development density
- Enhanced lease value generated by greater pedestrian volume
- Increased marketability to tenants/home-owners
- Improved access to labor markets
- Increased retail sales
- Reduced transportation costs for employees and employers

Employers...
- Improved employee morale
- Stable work force
- Improved attendance
- Aid to recruiting new employees
- Broadened work force

Pace highlights some of the advantages that transit offers to businesses.

1-5

employee benefits packages over those offered by competing employers. A study of the Bay Area Commuter Check program found that a large majority (79%) of respondents noted improved opinions of their employer as a result of receiving Commuter Checks, a third (35%) noted reduced stress from not driving to work or driving less often, and a third (33%) said job satisfaction had improved. Improvements in on-time arrival and productivity were also noted. Other advantages may be more subtle. For example, working to support environmentally friendly transportation solutions may improve a company's public image in certain markets. Although the benefits will vary with the setting, working with transit operators has clear-cut advantages for the business community. Businesses have ready access to a service that enhances their position in the marketplace – and can save them money in the process.

The Challenges

For decades, public transit has competed in an ever-more difficult market. Transit fares continue to rise, operating subsidies are being reduced, and ridership has declined in many markets. The competition is formidable. Gasoline prices have been stable or dropping in real terms for years. Suburbanization trends continue (although some communities are recognizing the costs of this trend and are working to reduce sprawl). Parking is often widely available, and air quality regulations affecting commuting (where they applied) have generally been eased. Moreover, the automobile industry easily outspends transit on marketing its product. In 1996, the auto industry spent $11.6 billion on advertising, which was more than 17 percent of all U.S. advertising dollars and nearly two-thirds of all transit operating expenditures that year.

> A study in the San Francisco Bay Area found that the increase in transit use as a result of employer-provided transit benefits was 48 percent at employers *outside* the city of San Francisco compared to 25 percent at employers *in* San Francisco. The greater increase in the suburbs suggests that transit subsidies can offset the influence of free or heavily subsidized parking.

Transit-to-business marketing can help offset these market imbalances. Accordingly, over the past ten years, transit-to-business marketing has changed from a peripheral concern to a major focus in many agencies. The business community offers many resources, including the ability to sponsor new services, support promotions, subsidize fares, provide in-kind staff support (employee transportation coordinators or executives on loan), and – of course – supply passengers. It is no wonder then, that over the past ten years, more and more transit agencies have begun to explore the possibilities for marketing their services directly to businesses.

To pursue this partnership, transit agencies often need to change their own way of doing business. Successful examples of business-to-business marketing have a number of characteristics in common. They all:

- Understand the customer
- Respond to customer needs
- Sell to the customer
- Provide leadership and support.

These four characteristics can be summarized into one simple concept: *Focus on the customer*. In most cases, the customer will be the employer (or other member of the business community). At other times, however, transit agencies may focus their business marketing efforts on riders – the end users – as a strategy to reach their employers. (This approach, known as rider-based marketing, will be discussed in subsequent chapters.) The ability to assess the customer's needs and quickly respond to them is an essential prerequisite to a successful business marketing program. Despite the apparent simplicity of this approach, it may represent a shift in perspective for some transit providers. And while this kind of change may not come easily to transit agencies, focusing on customers and their needs is the key to success with transit-to-business marketing.

How To Use This Report

This workbook is based on the findings of TCRP Study B-8, *Effective Methods of Marketing Transit Services to Business*. In addition to reviewing published material on both business-to-business and transit-to-business marketing techniques, the study surveyed leading transit agencies, convened a panel of individuals with expertise in the field, and took substantial direction from the TCRP panel guiding the study. Four case studies were performed. Two reviewed efforts of Bank of America and Kaiser Permanente to re-invent products and expand market share. The third examined the efforts of Pace, the suburban Chicago transit agency, to expand services to the business community and integrate business support for transit. The fourth case study reviewed recent national experience with transit voucher subsidy programs. Throughout the document, an attempt has been made to maximize the number of examples and illustrations of how transit-to-business and business-to-business marketing has actually worked.

Chapter 2 summarizes the lessons of business-to-business marketing, emphasizing the key elements of sales and institutional change. Chapters 3-5 present an approach for developing and implementing a transit-to-business marketing plan. Chapter 6 summarizes the findings.

Chapter 2

Lessons from the Marketplace

Overview

Selling transit services to business is much like selling any other product, from office supplies to health insurance. Successful business-to-business marketing techniques incorporate four basic elements:

- Understand the customer

- Respond to customer needs

- Sell to the customer

- Provide leadership and support.

These principles of business marketing can be divided into two general categories, which are amplified below: (1) product development, and (2) effective sales techniques.

Product Development

Understand the Customer

Marketing any product successfully relies on one fundamental principal: Understand the customer. The business community recognizes that there is no substitute for knowing what the customer wants; all subsequent decisions about product development and marketing should follow from this knowledge. Acquiring an understanding of customer needs generally involves some level of market research, which can range from large-scale telephone surveys to casual meetings in the employee cafeteria. Before developing new employer-based transit services, Pace may conduct a large-scale employee survey to assess transportation needs. In New York, the TransitChek program conducted a series of focus groups with personnel and benefits administrations to identify successful marketing strategies. And Bank of America surveyed its customers to test the effectiveness of the marketing campaign for a new checking account.

For many businesses, market research is the starting point for identifying customer needs. Research can be done locally or adapted from experience in other settings. The research may be narrowly focused (What is the best way to promote transit in a shopping center?) or it may be broad-based (What would encourage people to shift from driving to transit?). It may focus on employers, retailers, or developers. In some cases, existing riders, would-be riders, or former riders – the ultimate transit consumers – may be the subject of market research. No matter who makes up the target market, understanding what the customer wants is the first step toward meeting those needs.

> After making a corporate commitment to increase its lending to small business owners, Bank of America developed a series of products tailored to the needs of that specific market.

Respond to Customer Needs

Once market research has determined what customers want, a plan to address those needs must be developed. Sometimes a product or service meeting the stated need already exists, but customers do not know about it. Businesses unfamiliar with transit may not be aware of an agency's range of services, or they may recognize the benefits to them and their employees. In these cases, it is fairly easy for a transit provider to offer information about current services and good data about transit benefits for businesses, such as tax savings and increased productivity. More likely, however, a transit operator will have to develop a new product, or modify an existing one, in order to respond to customer needs. Some examples follow.

- When Sears, Roebuck relocated from downtown Chicago to suburban Hoffman Estates, Pace designed a series of subscription bus routes to transport employees to this new suburban location.

- In Connecticut, CT Transit improved service to two major retail centers in Hartford by rescheduling the last buses of the day to serve store employees commuting home.

- TransitChek was originally developed as a measure to overcome the complexity of administering a transit voucher program in a multi-operator environment.

Although they differ in cost and complexity, these examples illustrate the range of possible responses to specific customer needs.

Passenger boarding Pace subscription bus.

Effective Sales Techniques

Developing the product is only the first step in transit-to-business marketing – albeit a crucial one. Now the challenge is to sell that product, by assembling a motivated staff and providing them with the tools and support they need to get the job done. It is important to recognize that it is possible to take advantage of a sales force at any budget level. While some transit operators may have the resources to create a dedicated sales staff, others may decide instead to expand the responsibilities of existing staff or even to use riders as a "deputized sales force."

Sell to the Customer

Just as the product must be defined from the customer's perspective, effective sales efforts are also customer-defined. A skilled salesperson can identify a customer's key concerns and respond to them. By doing so, the sales staff is not selling the product – but selling a solution.

The most successful salesperson is the one who knows what it takes to close the deal – and will adapt the product, adapt the pitch, and even back off if necessary. For example, carpools and vanpools with fixed departure times may only appeal to a limited share of commuters (and even fewer employers), but adding a guaranteed ride home program can expand the market. Hourly bus headways may not be marketable to employers, but increasing headways during peak hours or at shift changes may be the critical selling point. A bus stop several blocks away may not be attractive enough to encourage a large employer to participate in a transit program, but delivering a new stop or modified route might make all the difference. Employers in larger cities may respond well to the tax advantages of providing transit benefits to their employees, while in smaller cities they may be more sensitive to the impacts on parking and employment issues. Developers may not initially appreciate the benefits of a building design that allows transit access to a suburban site, but a creative salesperson can assemble convincing data about the merits of transit-friendly design.

To guide marketing and sales efforts, marketing staff must be familiar with the market research defining customer needs and with successful past practices, either at their agency or elsewhere. Clear, attractive materials describing available programs, benefits, and success stories should be readily available to share with prospective customers as appropriate. These marketing materials can be printed, audiovisual, or electronic; the format is not important as long as they clearly identify products and benefits to the customer.

Good salespeople respond to customer concerns using all available resources. If they cannot solve a problem personally, they will find the person who can. Solving customer's problems on an individual basis may not be easy in the public sector, where bureaucracy can seem to slow every decision, but a motivated salesperson will do whatever it takes to close the deal.

Provide Leadership and Support

As an entrepreneurial activity, transit-to-business marketing can be difficult to foster in the public sector. Sometimes the procedural regulations and policies that govern public agencies do not easily accommodate the targeted approaches, quick turnaround, and flexible responses that are critical to marketing activities.

A successful transit-to-business marketing approach must incorporate both external and internal elements: a focus on the customer and a simultaneous organizational commitment to follow through. Not only must marketing staff be empowered to make deals that address the needs of their customers, but they must also have the authority to deliver a response. In most cases, this will call for a close and cooperative relationship with other groups within the transit agency. Examples of cross-department solutions include: working with planning and operations to implement reasonable changes in routes, delivering a bus shelter at a key location, tailoring a voucher program to meet company needs, and introducing a shoppers shuttle in return for a

Pace created a videotape to market its Vanpool Incentive Program.

Transit Cooperative Research Program

> **Public Sector Profit Sharing?**
>
> Unique in the transit industry (but very common elsewhere), a transit agency in Vermont has used a "revenue sharing plan" that has all agency staff receiving a pro-rated share of half of the excess fare revenue that the agency receives above the annually budgeted target. Begun as an experimental and informal marketing program (stimulated by rider survey results indicating that operator attitudes were a key element in service quality), it was so successful that the union requested that it become part of a renewed agreement. In its first year, 28 percent fewer operator complaints and 30 percent more commendations were received. Management also noted operator attention to fare collection duties improved, and that a "positive peer pressure" among operators developed.

commitment to subsidize a percentage of operating costs. But without the ability to deliver on a commitment, the sales staff – and, by extension, the transit agency – will have no credibility within the business community.

In many cases, fostering this level of coordination and cooperation will require some degree of organizational change. For some agencies, it may be a seemingly simple matter of communication and collaboration. After a marketing staffer promises to modify a bus schedule, for example, operations has to make it happen. At other times an agency may have to introduce internal systems changes to support its marketing activities. Kaiser Permanente actually linked its marketing and operations functions at the national and local levels, while Pace developed a new strategic planning group as part of an overall strategy to reinvent the agency. Bank of America modified its computer and accounting systems to support a new product, as did Pace, which introduced new bookkeeping procedures to bill vanpool customers directly for their monthly fares.

No matter what the level of institutional change required, it will require vision and leadership to ensure that all elements of the organization work to support the sales staff. An agency-wide agenda can provide the grounding and support to ensure appropriate follow-through. If an agency has clearly articulated goals for the marketing program – goals that are generally understood, accepted and supported throughout the agency – then the sales force will not work in isolation. Rather they will be able to collaborate with operations, financial, and other personnel as appropriate to ensure that the product they sold is actually delivered.

An expanded focus on business development may mean encouraging transit employees to try new approaches. Creating change can be difficult in a large organization, where there is at least as much opportunity to fail as there is to succeed. If the organization penalizes failure more than it rewards success, it is unlikely that change will be widely or actively pursued. Those who do will be the exceptions rather than members of a team pursuing shared ends. Organizations working to encourage innovation may find it effective to introduce incentives that support risk-taking among employees. Although sales incentives in the private sector are usually financial, there are ample opportunities in the transit industry to reward productive and innovative employees with praise, awards (Employee of the Month) and other non-monetary incentives. The entire organization can also share in the successes of every department to create an environment for teamwork.

A transit-to-business marketing program will not succeed if it is just a new name for business as usual. It cannot be the responsibility of one individual – or even one department. The program must represent a direction for the entire agency, and every employee must be a partner in the program.

> Bank of America unveiled a comprehensive employee training program to support its new Alpha account. The bank used video conferencing to reach branch employees across the state and distributed detailed guides that provided technical information about the account as well as ideas for promoting the service with clients.

Chapter 3

Getting Started

Overview

Developing an effective marketing plan requires five fundamental steps:

- Set goals
- Define the market
- Develop the product
- Select sales techniques
- Evaluate results

These are described in detail in the next three chapters.

Set Goals

Establishing a realistic set of goals is the first step in developing an effective marketing program. Goals should extend across the organization, and may incorporate targets for ridership and revenue, community and political standing, and institutional change. The process for setting these goals may involve market research, organizational review, strategic planning, and – for some operations – considerable soul-searching. No matter what the process, a thoughtful and comprehensive set of organizational goals will establish a framework for an effective marketing program.

The process of setting goals has two components:

- Organizational goals
- Program goals

Organizational goals are the big-picture goals: increase ridership, expand revenue sources, build political support. These goals define the organizational culture and they should infuse virtually every decision made throughout the agency, from the general manager to the bus operator. The role that institutional goals play in organizational change cannot be overstated; they can either inspire pursuit of new directions or foil such efforts.

Program goals are more specific than organizational goals. They need to be fully articulated, perhaps through research, and can include more detailed action statements. Program goals may focus on particular markets; they may have direct and indirect targets, and short- and long-term elements. Well-defined goal statements can be action plans that inspire an organization; poorly defined goals may lead to apathy or, worse, cynicism.

Pace's Marketing Plan establishes specific numeric targets for each market based on research findings. For example, after determining that 10 percent of its suburb-to-suburb commuters used Pace less than four days per week, Pace developed strategies to increase their utilization rates by one day per week.

Goal setting requires more than a vision or an idea – it requires quantifying target markets, the expected impacts and the costs of getting there. Without this, it is impossible to verify if the expected returns from any product proposal are large enough to justify the costs involved. For example, Bank of America has developed a strict planning process to help determine which products offer the greatest growth and profit potential; projects are prioritized based on the efforts and dollars needed to develop the business. Setting targets during the planning process can facilitate program evaluation after implementation.

Of course not all transit goals can be presented in quantifiable terms. While it may be possible to estimate ridership impacts and to calculate costs for some programs, other transit benefits may be difficult, or impossible, to quantify. In these cases it may be possible to estimate the number of new riders that would need to be generated to cover the program's costs. To do this, one must assume not only the number of new users, but also their riding frequency and the duration of that new ridership. This can allow comparisons between programs in order to assess how they relate to both organizational and program goals. For example, an agency might compare the value of advertising to encourage new passengers to take the bus to the mall on the day after Thanksgiving with a program that promotes new commuter trips. While each program might generate a similar number of riders, the commuter-oriented program might attract recurring work trips while the shopping promotion may attract one-time trips. This comparison can help illuminate the level of investment a new program can justify, whether through advertising, promotional materials, or staff time.

Define the Market

Market research is critical to understanding the needs of current and potential transit customers. Without reliable information on the market for its services, an agency cannot expect to implement effective programs; pursuing "seat of the pants" project design can be an extremely risky strategy. Market research techniques are well documented and will not be explored in this guidebook; they include written, telephone or personal surveys; focus groups; and product testing. However, it is important for transit agencies to recognize that a range of market research techniques is available at all budgets.

In addition to providing insights into the transit market, market research can help transit providers identify specific groups for targeted marketing strategies. Market segmentation is a technique for dividing the larger market into specific groups according to key characteristics and needs. For example, Pace subdivided its transit market into three groups: (1) suburb-to-city, (2) suburb-to-suburb, (3) city-to-suburb. In Seattle, King County Metro divides its customers by geographic residence and commuting mode.

Databases are an easy and often inexpensive way for organizations to generate lists of target businesses. Many transit organizations use internal databases created from years of experience working with employers, while others use commercially available databases such as those published by Dun & Bradstreet to reach smaller employers. Some agencies (particularly those that have been in operation longer) will maintain their own database. Seattle Metro targets employers that are not meeting the goals set out by the area's Commute Trip Reduction (CTR) law for special marketing efforts, with the intent to aid them in meeting their goals in the future.

Other unusual targeted marketing has been implemented in California and Florida. The San Diego Association of Governments designs potential vanpool routes, and then identifies major employers along the proposed route. These employers are then contacted directly and asked if they would be interested in encouraging their employees to participate in the proposed vanpool. The Miami Beach TMA is marketing a new shuttle service directly to the hotels and attractions in the area, who will then market the service individually to their guests as an alternative means of traveling to tourist sites. Near Tampa, Florida, the University North Transportation Initiative has used sophisticated statistical and Geographic Information System data to demonstrate to business leaders the depth of the transit and traffic problems they are facing, and to encourage them to buy into the solution process.

One particularly useful strategy may be to conduct research among former transit users, those who have decreased their usage, or those who do not use transit at all. These groups can yield valuable insights into customer preferences. For example, Bank of America surveyed customers who closed accounts, which could be likened to "former rider" studies. The bank conducted personal interviews with these former customers to assess their perceptions and reasons for leaving the bank. Kaiser Permanente restructured its market research program to evaluate repurchasing decisions among its members. In other words, the organization began to track whether existing customers chose to repurchase Kaiser health plans and whether they recommended the plan to others. Based on this research, Kaiser was able to identify the elements that separated "loyal" customers (those that repurchased coverage) from "disloyal" customers (those that purchased another health plan).

> Based on its research into customer purchase decisions, Kaiser Permanente divided its market into four categories:
> - **Low price.** Customers focused on the cost of service.
> - **"Give it to me straight, doc."** Clients interested in a no-frills approach to health care.
> - **High touch.** Customers valuing physician-patient relationship.
> - **"Crystals and wheat germ."** Clients interested in alternative and holistic therapies.

Once potential target groups have been identified, it is necessary to set priorities. Often it is most effective to target the easiest market first. For Pace, this meant focusing on Sears Roebuck & Company, which was relocating about 5,000 employees from downtown Chicago to suburban Hoffman Estates – an area with no transit service. For other providers the logical target markets may be employers for whom incremental service changes may address employee needs.

EMPLOYEE COMMUTE OPTIONS SURVEY

Dear Employee:
Your firm is conducting this survey to understand how employees travel to work. Please complete and return this survey to your company representative as soon as possible. You may use pencil or pen to complete this survey. ©Pace

NOTE: To answer a question, FILL IN THE BOX COMPLETELY. Proper Marks ■ ■ ■ ■   Improper Marks ☑ ☐ ⊠

1007929

Please fill in the information for your work trips for the five sampling days.

1. Please indicate whether you reported to your work site on each day.

	MON	TUES	WED	THUR	FRI
Yes	☐	☐	☐	☐	☐
No (Telecommuted)	☐	☐	☐	☐	☐
No (Vacation Day)	☐	☐	☐	☐	☐
No (Sick/Personal Day)	☐	☐	☐	☐	☐
No (Off-site Work)	☐	☐	☐	☐	☐
No (Other)	☐	☐	☐	☐	☐

2. For each day of the week, mark the top box for your scheduled beginning time, and mark the bottom box for your scheduled ending time. (Please indicate AM or PM.)

   SCHEDULED BEGINNING TIME (grid with hours 1–12 and minutes 00–55 for EXAMPLE, MON, TUES, WED, THUR, FRI, with AM/PM selection)

   SCHEDULED ENDING TIME (grid with hours 1–12 and minutes 00–55 for EXAMPLE, MON, TUES, WED, THUR, FRI, with AM/PM selection)

3. What was the primary (main) mode used to make your trip each day? (Mark only one per day.)

	MON	TUES	WED	THUR	FRI
Walked	☐	☐	☐	☐	☐
Drove a Car	☐	☐	☐	☐	☐
Carpooled	☐	☐	☐	☐	☐
Vanpooled	☐	☐	☐	☐	☐
Pace Bus	☐	☐	☐	☐	☐
CTA Bus	☐	☐	☐	☐	☐
CTA Train	☐	☐	☐	☐	☐
Metra Train	☐	☐	☐	☐	☐
Rode Bicycle	☐	☐	☐	☐	☐
Rode Motorcycle	☐	☐	☐	☐	☐
Did Not Make Trip	☐	☐	☐	☐	☐
Other	☐	☐	☐	☐	☐

   — Next Column —

4. If you traveled in a vehicle by yourself for part of your trip to work, how far did you travel in this vehicle?

	MON	TUES	WED	THUR	FRI
Under 1 Mile	☐	☐	☐	☐	☐
1-4 Miles	☐	☐	☐	☐	☐
5-9 Miles	☐	☐	☐	☐	☐
10-24 Miles	☐	☐	☐	☐	☐
Over 24 Miles	☐	☐	☐	☐	☐
Does Not Apply	☐	☐	☐	☐	☐

5. If you rode in a bus or train for part of your trip to work, how far did you travel in these vehicles?

	MON	TUES	WED	THUR	FRI
Under 1 Mile	☐	☐	☐	☐	☐
1-4 Miles	☐	☐	☐	☐	☐
5-9 Miles	☐	☐	☐	☐	☐
10-24 Miles	☐	☐	☐	☐	☐
Over 24 Miles	☐	☐	☐	☐	☐
Does Not Apply	☐	☐	☐	☐	☐

6. If you rode in a carpool or vanpool for part of your trip to work, how far did you travel in this vehicle?

	MON	TUES	WED	THUR	FRI
Under 1 Mile	☐	☐	☐	☐	☐
1-4 Miles	☐	☐	☐	☐	☐
5-9 Miles	☐	☐	☐	☐	☐
10-24 Miles	☐	☐	☐	☐	☐
Over 24 Miles	☐	☐	☐	☐	☐
Does Not Apply	☐	☐	☐	☐	☐

7. If you rode in a carpool or vanpool, were you the main driver?
   ☐ Yes, I drove   ☐ No, I was the rider

8. How many persons, including yourself, were in the auto, carpool, or vanpool? (Exclude children unless they are going to work as employees.)

	MON	TUES	WED	THUR	FRI
Just Myself	☐	☐	☐	☐	☐
2 Persons	☐	☐	☐	☐	☐
3 Persons	☐	☐	☐	☐	☐
4 Persons	☐	☐	☐	☐	☐
5 Persons	☐	☐	☐	☐	☐
6 Persons	☐	☐	☐	☐	☐
7 Persons	☐	☐	☐	☐	☐
8 Persons	☐	☐	☐	☐	☐
9 Persons	☐	☐	☐	☐	☐
10 Persons	☐	☐	☐	☐	☐
11 Persons	☐	☐	☐	☐	☐
12 Persons	☐	☐	☐	☐	☐
13 Persons	☐	☐	☐	☐	☐
14 Persons	☐	☐	☐	☐	☐
15 Persons	☐	☐	☐	☐	☐

9. While driving, did you stop on your way to or from work, and did you need your car during work hours? (Mark all that apply.)

	MON	TUES	WED	THUR	FRI
Yes (To or From Work)	☐	☐	☐	☐	☐
No (To or From Work)	☐	☐	☐	☐	☐
Yes (During Work Hours)	☐	☐	☐	☐	☐
Does Not Apply	☐	☐	☐	☐	☐

   — Over —

SCANTRON FORM NO. F-4910-PACE © SCANTRON CORPORATION 1993 ALL RIGHTS RESERVED

Pace conducts employee surveys to help employers assess their transportation needs.

Marketing Transit Services to Business

10. If you stopped, where did you stop? (Mark all that apply.)

	MON	TUES	WED	THUR	FRI
Work-Related	☐	☐	☐	☐	☐
Social/Recreational	☐	☐	☐	☐	☐
School	☐	☐	☐	☐	☐
Day Care	☐	☐	☐	☐	☐
Banking	☐	☐	☐	☐	☐
Grocery Store	☐	☐	☐	☐	☐
Other	☐	☐	☐	☐	☐

11. What is your home city and zip code?

    City/Village: _____

    ZIP CODE | +4 (If Known)
    (bubble grid 0–9)

12. For each day of the week, please mark the box for when you began your trip to work.
    (Please indicate AM or PM.)

    BEGINNING OF TRIP
    EXAMPLE | MON | TUES | WED | THUR | FRI
    (AM/PM, HR, MIN bubble grid)

13. Did you work a compressed work week?
    - ☐ Yes, I worked a 4-day, 40-hour compressed work week.
    - ☐ Yes, I worked a 3-day, 40-hour compressed work week.
    - ☐ Yes, I worked a 9-day, 80-hour compressed work schedule.
    - ☐ No, I worked a 5- or 6-day or "regular" work week.
    - ☐ No, I worked less than 17 hours this week.
    - ☐ No, other

14. Would you use a park-and-ride lot located near your home if a ride-sharing service went from the park-and-ride lot to your firm?
    - ☐ Probably Would Use
    - ☐ Might Use
    - ☐ Probably Would Not Use

-- Next Column --

Pace offers the following transportation options. Please indicate how likely you would be to use each of these services for traveling to work if they were available.

Fixed Route: A regular bus service that follows a defined route.

Express Route: A premium bus service that collects riders and then travels non-stop on a highway to an employment center.

Subscription Route: A premium bus service that collects riders and then travels non-stop to work. Pre-payment is required.

Reverse Feeder: A bus service that goes from a Metra rail station to a group of firms.

Vanpool: A group of riders sharing a ride to work in a van. One of the members drives the van. The others pay a monthly fee.

	WOULD DEFINITELY USE	WOULD PROBABLY USE	MIGHT USE	WOULD PROBABLY NOT USE	WOULD DEFINITELY NOT USE
15. Fixed Route	☐	☐	☐	☐	☐
16. Express Route	☐	☐	☐	☐	☐
17. Subscription	☐	☐	☐	☐	☐
18. Reverse Feeder	☐	☐	☐	☐	☐
19. Vanpool	☐	☐	☐	☐	☐

20. If you could not drive to work everyday, what would be your first, second, and third choices as employee commute options? (Select only 3.)

	CHOICES		
	1st	2nd	3rd
Walking	☐	☐	☐
Bicycling	☐	☐	☐
Carpooling	☐	☐	☐
Vanpooling	☐	☐	☐
Riding Metra Train	☐	☐	☐
Riding Pace Bus	☐	☐	☐
Riding CTA Train	☐	☐	☐
Riding CTA Bus	☐	☐	☐
Telecommuting	☐	☐	☐
4-Day, Compressed Week	☐	☐	☐
9-Day, 80-Hour Compressed Schedule	☐	☐	☐
Other	☐	☐	☐

21. Please indicate your gender.   ☐ Male   ☐ Female

    Comments: _____
    _____
    _____
    _____

Thank you. Please return this survey to your company representative as soon as possible.

Administrative Use Only:

Site Code: Ⓐ Ⓑ Ⓒ Ⓓ Ⓔ Ⓕ

Once a target market has been established, an agency can build on its success with early participants to sell later ones, who may fear that other employers are better serving their customers and/or employees. Employers have been seen to be very competitive about maintaining the attractiveness of their benefits policies. This kind of competition can be a powerful motivating force for selling transit services to businesses.

Develop the Product

The steps to this point may represent business as usual for many transit agencies. Most agencies routinely undertake some form of market research and most have mission statements describing agency-wide goals. Linking these general goals to targeted marketing and especially to product development, however, may require a new way of thinking about transit services.

> Research has shown that many auto commuters make stops between home and work. To encourage these commuters to switch modes, more incentives for occasional use of transit might be developed (such as deeply discounted multi-ride tickets). Or *SuperTransfers* or *Extend-a-Ride* fare instruments can be used to allow re-boarding without paying multiple fares.

Once one or more target markets have been selected, the transit provider must identify customer needs. This needs assessment should be as detailed as possible, because it will form the basis for developing transit programs and services. Research again is the key to identifying specific customer needs. Typical strategies include employee surveys, interviews with management, and on-site meetings with commuters. Pace spent months meeting with Sears employees in order to assess commuting patterns and mode preferences. Bank of America conducted personal interviews with potential customers in order to design its Alpha Account, while TransitChek has made extensive use of focus groups to help refine the concept and final design for its product.

No matter what the product, it must solve a problem for the customer. Customers do not buy products to solve a problem they do not recognize, nor do they buy products that solve someone else's problem. While good marketing may motivate people to try transit, only good service can keep them as users. Again, this is where market research can provide insights that can help ensure long-term success. Sometimes one feature emerges from the research process to become the critical design element in the new product. Customers may be looking for a product that offers **high value**, such as a guaranteed ride home program or Denver's EcoPass program, which makes deeply discounted transit passes available to employers who purchase them for all employees. TransitChek was developed to bring **simplicity** to the process of administering a transit benefit program in a multi-operator environment. Bank of America designed new banking features to maximize customer **choice**. Some programs focus on **flexibility**, as seen in King County Metro's voucher programs and Bank of America's new services for small business. Finally, based on market research that similarly surfaced the desire for discounts and perceived value, Milwaukee County Transit offered a sharply discounted monthly pass plan only through employers who provide a matching discount. In this case, *not* providing the product to the general market yields a perception of **special value** for the participating employers.

For some products, research can play a critical role in product design and may, in fact, determine the success or failure of a marketing program. New York's transit voucher program began with a goal of offsetting subsidies for auto users; research had found that these subsidies were a key factor motivating commuters to drive into Manhattan. At first, the voucher concept was considered "exotic" relative to conventional approaches like token sales, pass handling, passes-by-mail, or reimbursements. Yet when various alternatives for providing fare subsidies were tested in focus groups of personnel and benefit managers, only the voucher got strong endorsement. Managers saw it as a streamlined option matching their need to minimize benefits administration staffing requirements. The market's strong endorsement of this once exotic idea led to a much broader planning effort and procurement of a major grant to support the program's introduction.

Finally, market research can help reveal the most effective strategies for marketing a product. In TransitChek's New York focus groups, personnel managers said that employee pressure would be the most important factor in motivating their company to adopt a new transit benefit plan. This insight changed the early planning of New York's TransitChek marketing from a sole focus on business-to-business direct mail to a rider-based approach with some direct mail.

King County Metro's pass program stresses flexibility.

What is a FlexPass?
FlexPass offers employees daily access to many commute options. Metro and the employer work together to offer specific transportation services to employees through the FlexPass program.

The FlexPass program typically includes full access to Metro transit services, ridematch services, Home Free Guarantee, vanpool fare subsidies and free or reduced rate carpool or vanpool parking. The package may also include park-free days, merchant discount programs, voucher programs or other strategies tailored to the worksite. Having access to many transit benefits increases employees' flexibility when they choose their daily commute mode. It also increases the likelihood of a successful FlexPass program.

"The FlexPass program at Bristol Meyers Squibb adds much more flexibility to my commute. Even though I drive to work, mid-day errands are much easier. I know that I can jump on Metro and reach downtown."

Larry Benedict, Bristol Meyers Squibb

What are the benefits of a FlexPass?
To employers:
- can reduce transportation program or facilities costs due to discounted transit benefits and a reduced need for employee parking spaces
- permits equity of transportation benefits among employees
- offers a visible demonstration of corporate support and leadership
- provides a proven way to encourage employees to use alternative types of transportation
- offers easy program administration.

To employees:
- offers flexibility in daily commute mode choice
- provides low or no cost transportation benefits
- allows full access to all FlexPass benefits such as ridematching, Home Free Guarantee and other incentives.

What are favorable characteristics or conditions for FlexPass?
FlexPass is most effective when:
- employees use many types of transportation to commute
- employer charges for or limits parking
- transit operates within ¼ mile of the employment site or an employee group coordinates and uses carpools or vanpools to commute
- employer is willing to provides incentives such as a guaranteed ride home program, a transit subsidy or preferential or discounted parking for employees.

Chapter 4

Tools and Techniques

Overview

This section discusses the communications strategies associated with marketing transit services to business. Typical techniques include the following:

- Direct sales

- Personal selling

- Rider-based marketing

- Partnerships

- Advertising and publicity

The range of applicable techniques will vary widely with the specific product and available budget. Major communications methods for transit-to-business marketing are listed on Table 4-1, and Table 4-2 notes primary marketing activities for each transit-to-business program.

Key factors that have determined the choice of marketing strategy and techniques used in various cities include available staff and budget resources, the level and type of support from participating transit operators, and the overall priority assigned to making the program grow. In general, though, most organizations contacted in the first phase of this project (which covered the full range of business-to-business marketing strategies) reported that they have used direct mail and telemarketing to make initial contact and to provide clients with more follow up information, while the use of business databases to segment the market and to target potential customers has been particularly effective. Organizations also use newsletters, informational pamphlets, and special promotional activities first to entice companies, then to keep participating companies informed. Also, a number of organizations stated that networking and word-of-mouth were the two most successful marketing techniques they had employed.

Most organizations agreed that personal contact is more effective at generating a response than direct mail or telemarketing, although the costs of face-to-face sales are considerably higher. Some sales staff will make personal visits, as well as provide on-site services to plan and implement promotional programs for transportation services. In Seattle, King County Metro uses two levels of marketing personnel to promote their transportation services. The first level, called Employee Transportation Representatives, is the front-line sales force, who make the initial contact to employers. This first level also works with employers to help them decide on which services to use. Once an employer is involved with Metro, individual technical specialists are available to assist in implementing particular services on a nuts-and-bolts level.

Table 4-1
Primary Communications Methods for Transit-Business Marketing

Strategy	Communications Methods
Personal Sales	Sales staff visit to key sites, transportation fairs, employee transportation coordinators
Direct Sales	Direct mail to businesses in target areas or business categories, telemarketing, electronic communications
Site-based	Posters for employee bulletin boards, flyers for employee stores or paycheck stuffers, company newsletters
Rider-based	Bus and train posters with tear-off slips, posters in stations, displays at customer service centers, driver handouts (in some cities, driver incentives are used)
Partnerships	Media or corporate sponsorship of programs or services
Publicity	News stories, press conferences, articles in newsletters of allied organizations
Advertising	Paid ads for radio, television, newspapers, newsletters

Table 4-2
Key Marketing Methods for Transit-to-Business Activities

Primary Marketing Activities

Action	Sales	Direct Mail	Rider-Based	Planning	TMA Support	PR	Institutional Support	On-Site	Technical Support	Sponsorship	Print	Media	Institutional Development	Institutional Coordination
On-site pass sales	✓		✓					✓						
Pass subsidies	✓		✓			✓		✓						
University Pass / ECOPASS Programs	✓		✓			✓	✓	✓						
Vouchers	✓	✓	✓			✓	✓			✓				
Credit card / Third-party billing	✓	✓												
Carpooling/Vanpooling	✓	✓						✓						
Guaranteed ride home	✓	✓						✓						
Employee transportation coordinators	✓				✓									
Transportation management associations							✓						✓	
Shuttle services	✓			✓										
Circulator services	✓			✓										
Subscription services	✓			✓										
Reverse commute services	✓	✓		✓										
Refining existing services	✓			✓										
Transit enhancements/Amenities	✓			✓										
Site design initiatives	✓													✓
Employer survey assistance	✓								✓					
Relocation services	✓													
Employee orientation materials	✓								✓		✓			
Transit information services	✓								✓					
Retail incentives	✓										✓	✓		
Sponsorship (media, corporate)	✓													
Regulatory initiatives														✓

Guaranteed Ride Home programs provide commuting flexibility.

A number of transit providers also market their programs and services by networking with politicians and business leaders, using existing and new relationships to make businesses aware of available products. Some agencies have found success by holding breakfasts and luncheons for participating businesses, primarily to recognize achievements, but also to give business leaders an opportunity to interact with representatives from the local transit agencies. Business associations and chambers of commerce have also been effective conduits for making businesses aware of transit services. Many providers also develop networks of what are often referred to as Employee Transportation Coordinators (ETCs), who function as representatives at an employment site and encourage their fellow employees to use the various services offered by the transit agency. ETC training programs have also been developed, and some transportation demand management regulations require ETC certification. Some agencies even offer programs for employers and employees to familiarize them with transit services and to provide an overview of possible benefits created by the use of public transportation.

Transit agencies also use television, radio, and print advertising to publicize their products and services, along with in-vehicle posters and placards. Providers also utilize a wide range of promotional materials to advertise their message, including newsletters, handouts, seat drops, videos, and pamphlets. A growing number of transit providers have branched out into the Internet, but it is still unclear whether this is an effective strategy for reaching the business market. Finally, many transit providers have taken advantage of a range of partnerships, including media sponsorship, endorsements, and co-marketing programs.

> Pace developed a comprehensive relocation package designed to address the needs of employers in its service area. Elements included:
> ❶ Development guidelines.
> ❷ Site plan review.
> ❸ Employee commuting surveys.
> ❹ On-site transit days.
> ❺ Customized transit services.

A well-structured communications plan is necessary, which may have both general market and target market elements. It would integrate all of the resources available, which for transit likely includes some no-cost actions (like press releases), low-cost actions (like rider-driven methods) as well as paid marketing efforts and maybe cooperative/leverage/sponsor efforts. The communications plan should detail printed requirements, media services, phases, out-bound marketing efforts, response activities, and other elements necessary for the specific product or program. While it is surely subject to change and updating, a written communications plan brings a focus to the various marketing requirements and schedules and helps ensure effective program implementation.

One example of comprehensive marketing approach is at the Virginia Department of Rail and Public Transportation (VDRPT). The department embarked on a multi-year campaign to market public transportation services throughout northern Virginia. The VDRPT campaign developed a comprehensive marketing strategy based on market research of area businesses. Basic market research and focus groups developed the information that served as the program's foundation. VDRPT first identified the transit programs most important to businesses and then developed a campaign to make companies aware of these services. The marketing campaign strategy focused on the use of personal selling by representatives from the TMAs and rideshare agencies in the area, with some use of direct mail to make initial contacts and to publicize programs to the general public. A Guaranteed Ride Home (GRH) program was also developed; the businesses surveyed stated that this element could make transit more attractive to them and to their employees. The campaign also included full-page ads in the business press as well as ads on local CNN broadcasts. Breakfasts were also planned at the Washington Press Club for CEOs and political leaders, along with the development of a speaker's bureau to organize presentations to publicize the program.

Direct Sales

Direct sales techniques are commonly used to contact potential customers, provide them with information about a product or service, and develop sales leads. Particular techniques include direct mail, telemarketing and, increasingly, electronic communications media like faxes or the Internet.

Direct Mail

Direct mail can be an effective way of marketing transit services to a targeted group. Potential customers are mailed information about a product and are given a means of asking for more information, of contacting a salesperson, or placing an order. As discussed earlier, many organizations find it particularly effective to maintain databases for key market segments, such as employers in a certain industry or geographic area. The Indianapolis Public Transportation Corporation operates a set of reverse commute services known as MetroWorks, which were created and funded in partnership with suburban businesses requiring more late night service to their locations. MetroWorks has been marketed using direct mail targeted at ZIP codes in the areas where service is provided. In the San Diego area, the Metropolitan Transit Development Board identifies areas of high potential transit ridership based on distribution of socioeconomic factors. Within these targeted corridors, surveys are conducted to identify issues and concerns that might affect ridership. MTDB uses the survey findings to tailor marketing materials for distribution to households in the targeted corridor. If surveyed residents expressed concerns about safety, the marketing materials might stress the system's security measures. The mailing also includes information about transit services in the area as well as a free round-trip ticket as an incentive to use the system. In Boston and San Francisco, the Commuter Check program sent a detailed brochure to downtown employers in targeted industries explaining how fare subsidies can cost less to provide than comparable salary increases. Finally, some agencies take advantage of mass mailings from other agencies or utilities to distribute information about their programs. For example, as part of its focus on small employers, TransitChek inserted a flyer into quarterly statements sent by the U.S. Department of Labor concerning unemployment insurance.

Telemarketing

Telemarketing is well suited for business-to-business marketing because business buyers can be contacted during regular business hours and are more likely to listen to a marketing pitch than consumers at home. Kaiser Permanente, for example, has used highly trained telemarketers to pave the way for a visit from a salesperson. This is also consistent with the New York TransitChek's sales efforts for larger employers.

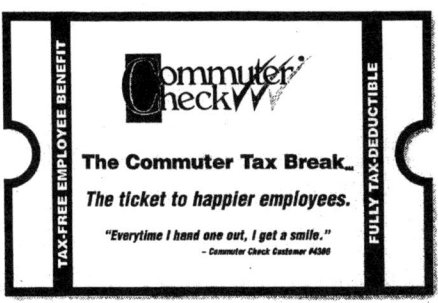

The Bay Area Commuter Check program mailed this postcard to targeted employers.

San Francisco International Airport used direct mail to promote ridesharing activities.

Electronic Communications

Some organizations have begun to take advantage of the Internet and facsimile communications to market their services. Like their private sector counterparts, many transit agencies maintain home pages on the Internet to present information about services, fares, schedules, and special events. While some sites simply present information, others are interactive. The Commuter Store in Arlington County, Virginia, allows passengers to purchase transit passes on-line; after submitting an order, passengers are transferred to a secure server where they can enter credit card information. CARAVAN for Commuters, a Boston-area ridesharing organization, posts a sign-up form for potential vanpool passengers and lists vanpools that have openings. Bank of America has used its Internet web site to provide information as well as personalized support using its "Build Your Own Bank" package. Customers design a personalized banking service by selected the features they prefer – from checking account options to investment products. Before customers can design their own bank account, however, they must complete a personal profile. Bank of America downloads this information into a database for future marketing purposes.

The Washington Metropolitan Transit Authority recently announced TripFax, a service available 24 hours a day offering bus and rail schedules by fax. The fully automated system allows requests for up to three schedules via recorded message prompts. Another innovative communications tool is the "mass fax" activity that notifies selected large employers of transit service disruptions in New York.

Rider-Based Marketing

Transit agencies should not overlook the advantages of using word-of-mouth as a marketing technique. Even when the target of a marketing campaign is business, this type of consumer-based marketing can play a role. For example, the New York TransitChek program initially believed that transit vouchers were a classic business-to-business product, and that the primary market was medium and large employers. This led program staff to use direct mail to employers with appropriate Standard Industrial Classification (SIC) Codes. The results were quite good but, unfortunately, the success came at a very high cost. Paid advertising in business publications yielded a very poor response, even when ads were included in special issues focused on employee benefits.

As the program expanded, it became clear that interest was greatest among small employers and that the best way to reach this large market was by communicating with the even larger market of transit users. It was seen that a critical factor driving employer enrollment in any new benefit plan was the demonstration of employee interest in the program. In fact, a series of focus groups with personnel and benefits administrators revealed that employers were more likely to respond to requests from their employees than to other direct marketing techniques. This insight helped frame the marketing plan for the New York TransitChek program, which evolved to rely increasingly on rider-driven methods such as bus and train posters, hand-outs and take-ones.

Using transit riders as an effective sales force has succeeded repeatedly in other large cities. These cities have extended rider-based methods used in New York to include actions such as ads in bus schedules, handouts in transit stations, electronic signs, station posters, and seat drops. Incentives have also been used to reward driver hand-out efforts, such as those used by Denver RTD and AC Transit to market their Commuter Check programs. It is notable that rider-driven methods have been effective only in larger cities, and of limited impact where transit has a small market share (Louisville, Buffalo, Norfolk). In smaller cities where bus riders could not be effective advocates for the program, the rider-driven method has not proven as successful.

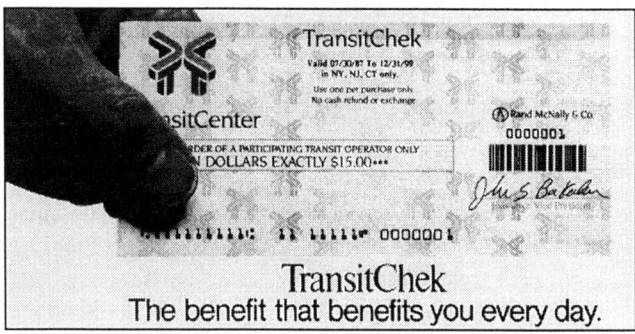

New York's TransitChek program markets directly to riders.

Personal Selling

Personal selling includes any direct contact between a transit agency and an employer. Contact may include meetings to present product information, on-site events like transportation fairs, or participation in community or civic organizations. In Chicago, Pace works with real estate agents to encourage transit use at existing multi-tenant facilities and to encourage transit-friendly design in new developments. Seattle Metro organizes network groups where employers with similar characteristics in the same geographic area are presented with product information simultaneously. By speaking to a number of businesses at the same time, the agency can justify more frequent interaction with employers, leading to an improved working relationship.

Sales Force

Perhaps the greatest difference between transit and private industry is in the area of sales. Private businesses routinely use sales staff to sell their products or services, while transit agencies rarely have the resources to do so. Nevertheless, a dedicated sales force can be very helpful for fostering interest in a service and for explaining the finer and more complex points of a program.

There are numerous models for organizing a sales force. One that may have applicability to transit is an "account executive" approach, where transit marketing staff develop ongoing personal relationships with their clients and customers. A geography-based approach may be appropriate, enabling transit managers to work with businesses within a defined geographic area. Pace has adopted this approach in its Marketing and Business Development Group. Each sales manager has a territory – much like a manufacturer's representative might have – and he or she is responsible for working with the employers and other businesses in that geographic area. Another approach may be to organize sales staff according to type of business. The business community is quite broad, and what works for one segment may not succeed with another. For example, one staff member may work with employers, another with educational institutions, still another with hospitals.

One of the greatest benefits of this approach is the single point of contact with the transit agency, often described as "one-stop shopping." Many local government agencies have introduced this concept to help eliminate red tape

Who is the business community?

- Employers
- Retailers
- Developers
- Business associations
- Government
- Hospitals
- Universities
- Nonprofits
- Media

> Bank of America introduced a Relationship Team to address the needs of its medium-sized business customers. The team comprises a Relationship Manager and representatives from other banking divisions. The Relationship Manager serves as the point of contact with the bank, providing a personal connection, and coordinates other activities.

with their development review and permitting functions. But transit agencies have sometimes been slow to adopt a similar approach. In some cases, businesses already work with transit agencies on a variety of issues, such as monthly pass sales, site review, and schedule modifications. If each of these efforts involve different personnel and there is little coordination, then the business is likely to experience frustration and a diminished desire to work together. Assigning a single person within the transit agency as the point of contact with a particular business enterprise could simplify matters for both organizations. Providing one-stop shopping for transit services and products saves time, money, and aggravation for businesses; channeling the concerns of a particular business through a single transit employee can enable the agency to see the big picture of what the business wants.

Networking

Networking with business leaders is another marketing technique used by many transit organizations. In some cases, this takes the form of directly contacting business leaders (sometimes using political or community leaders as an initial contact to reach the business leader). In other cases, agencies will coordinate meetings, seminars, and workshops where potential participants can hear about the positive experiences of current participants, as well as general information about particular services. This type of personal contact at higher levels of management gives information to individuals with the power to make the decisions necessary to involve their respective businesses in a given program.

Personal Meetings with Decision-Makers

Personal meetings with decision-makers at an employment site is an extremely important aspect of a marketing campaign because this is often where employers will make final decisions about program participation. Different agencies use different techniques for making direct contact with employers, depending in large part on agency size and funding. Small or poorly funded agencies may rely on technical staff to make initial presentations on various services. As described earlier, agencies with greater resources tend to have a dedicated sales staff, usually known as account representatives or account executives. This staff is in charge of all sales contact with potential customers ranging from the initial mailing or phone call all the way to the decision to participate. Once an employer has agreed to participate in the program, the sales force will act as a general resource, by answering questions, organizing events (such as a transportation fair), and keeping employers aware of new developments through regular mailings and phone calls.

> The American Public Transit Association sponsors the annual "Try Transit Week," where transit agencies set up transportation fairs to highlight their services.

Transportation Fairs

One very effective marketing technique used by transit organizations is the transportation fair, similar to the "health fairs" used by health insurance industry. For a transportation fair, a transit organization will arrange to set up a series of displays and information booths for employees at a particular location, usually in a building lobby or cafeteria. The displays will provide information about the various transportation services and their potential benefits to the user and to local communities, and can include items such as bus schedules, rideshare matching sign-up, information on biking or walking, as well as promotional materials. With recent advances in portable computing, it has even become possible to perform rideshare matching functions during the fair by showing

Marketing Transit Services to Business

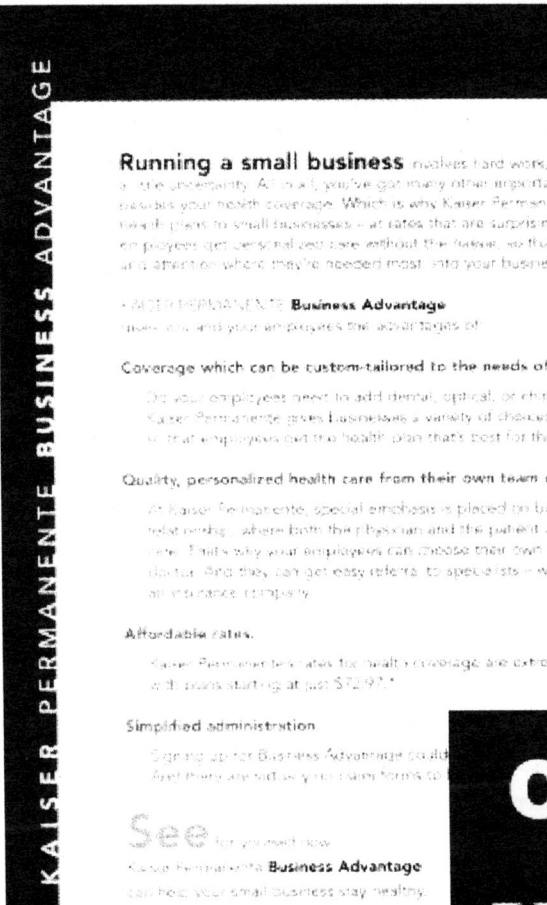

Business oriented marketing materials from Kaiser Permanente and Capital District Transportation Authority.

Guidelines for Sales Staff Training and Development

Choosing the right people for sales positions is critical, as is providing them with the training and tools they need to do their job.

Demeanor and approach. Despite evidence to the contrary, some businesses may harbor negative stereotypes of transit providers or government agencies in general. Clear guidelines on appearance and approach can help the sales force to dispel these stereotypes.

Listening to customer needs. Listening to customer needs can help the transit agency develop customized products that respond to specific identified needs and problems.

Available products. As the principal point of contact between the business community and the transit agency, the sales agencies must be familiar with the range of transit products available to the business community – from service hours to fare media.

Product benefits. Knowing *how* transit products can help a customer can help seal the deal. Knowing the impact on the customer's bottom line is even better. For example, the sales staff should be familiar with the tax benefits of a voucher program as well as the potential it has to increase ridership.

Good materials. Clear and attractive brochures, flyers, audiovisual presentations, and similar materials designed to give the impression of a serious and professional organization are a key element of success.

Close the deal. Successful operations give the sales staff the flexibility and support they need to work with colleagues in all parts of the transit organization in order to close the deal.

Providing feedback from the field can help fine-tune a product. For example, is a bus route too crowded? Does it run late enough or early enough to meet employer shifts?

Incentives. Finally, a successful sales program likely includes incentives for outstanding employees. This may include recognition, advancement, awards or bonuses for especially productive employees.

employees various ridesharing possibilities. In order to set up a fair at an employment site, a transit organization must deal directly with a decision-maker within the target organization. Because of this employer coordination, transportation fairs are an effective method for getting employers involved in encouraging their employees to use transit services.

Employee Transit Representatives

Many transportation management associations (TMAs) train and support a team of employee transportation coordinators to market their services. ETCs can work full- or part-time, or volunteer workers (with a salary paid by the employer, not the TMA), who are located at an employment site, and who will act as a central clearinghouse for all information about transportation programs and services. The ETCs are an on-site resource to management and employees, and who help market the services provided by the TMA and other alternative transportation providers.

Employee transportation coordinators can distribute transit passes on site.

Transit Courses

In Phoenix, the Regional Public Transportation Authority has found success in running introductory, so-called "Transit 101" classes to introduce employee contacts to riding public transit. This gives employees an opportunity to first gain experience with riding public transit, and then to pass that experience along to coworkers. By providing this advice and guidance, the Authority is able to encourage increased public transit usage while at the same time training more knowledgeable transit riders. A Washington, D.C., program operated by WMATA also has relied on group seminars to explain employee pass programs to interested employers. As one part of a comprehensive marketing program, these seminars can be particularly effective in reaching large employers.

Peer-to-Peer Sales

Such groupings encourage businesses to share experiences and offer advice. These groupings are also effective because they place experienced users in the position of selling transit or ridesharing programs to other business. This type of peer-to-peer sales is a proven strategy that encourages participation. Many successful TMAs incorporate this strategy; it recognizes that few employers want to be too far ahead or behind what their peers are doing for employee transportation issues.

Partnerships

Transit providers have found that partnerships with the business community can provide mutual benefits. Opportunities include sponsorship, co-marketing (also called co-branding), coordinated promotions, and endorsements. Many transit operators have pursued joint marketing programs with downtown shopping districts, suburban malls, sports facilities, and cultural institutions; they may offer coupons, incentives, or other forms of encouragement to consider transit.

Above: A local television station sponsored TARC's Commuter Check program.

Below: Denver RTD and Pace both have special promotions for sporting events.

Program Sponsorship

Numerous cities have gained free or discounted television advertising for their voucher programs in exchange for crediting the station as a sponsor. The San Francisco Bay Area Commuter Check program places its television station sponsor's logo on its marketing materials; in exchange, the station provides television coverage for the program. The mass marketing and product validation has considerable value to the local media outlets (who have their call letters on program brochures, flyers, and posters). For the voucher program, this approach has benefits that go beyond the greatly expanded advertising reach. This approach also provides an effective endorsement of the program that helped diminish initial reluctance in the business community about the long-term stability of a public sector program. The same can be said for letters of endorsement for new transit benefit programs from governors, mayors, leading employers, or business groups. Employers are unlikely to introduce employee benefit programs they fear are grant-based or otherwise short-lived.

Many transit operators take part in other types of sponsored programs that have applications for transit-to-business marketing. For example, in Boston, the Massachusetts Bay Transportation Authority offers a number of special offers to passengers who purchase monthly passes. Passholders are eligible to receive a discount on their automobile insurance; a number of area museums and tourist attractions offer discounts to passholders as well.

Providing service to special events can be another opportunity to market transit services. NJ TRANSIT works with various cultural institutions to offer special packages; for example, patrons can receive free transportation when they purchase tickets for selected Broadway musicals or performances in local theaters. In Denver, RTD provides game-day service for the Colorado Rockies and Denver Broncos from numerous locations throughout the metropolitan area. Finally, transit agencies can work with area businesses to generate their own special events. In Connecticut, the Greater Bridgeport Transit District sponsored a fare-free day on Columbus Day; a local bank agreed to cover lost revenues. A local radio station cosponsored the event and donated extensive promotional efforts. The event was so successful that the transit operator worked with another bank to follow up with another free ride day on the day after Thanksgiving.

Coordinated Promotions

Areas with constrained marketing budgets have successfully integrated marketing for transit programs with related activities. Transportation Management Associations (TMAs), for example, can actively market transit services or voucher programs along with rideshare services and other TDM activities. The San Francisco Commuter Check program had marketing support from RIDES for Bay Area Commuters (the regional ridesharing service), which promoted the program through its general employer outreach and local TMA support efforts. Connecticut's Metropool and Long Island's Ridesharing have also promoted the voucher program TransitChek in the New York suburbs, while CARAVAN for Commuters has supported marketing efforts for Boston's Commuter Check program. Also in Boston, the Massachusetts Bay

Marketing Transit Services to Business

Transportation Authority participates in SmarTraveler, a program that provides telephone callers with free up-to-the-minute reports on travel conditions throughout the metropolitan area; traffic reporters will mention transit as an alternative when local highways are congested.

Advertising and Publicity

While advertising and publicity campaigns are primarily directed at transit consumers, they also have transit-to-business applications. Most general advertising is aimed at employees in hopes that they will convince their respective companies to enroll in a transit program. Transit providers have used a wide range of techniques to market their services. While print and broadcast media advertisements are by far the most common, other techniques include newsletters, videotapes promoting products and services, and special promotional efforts such as prize giveaways and letters aimed at employees.

Media Advertising

Some organizations have been quite creative in advertising their services, and have even designed their own innovative campaigns. The TMO Metropool, in Stamford, Connecticut, is planning a campaign modeled after the "Dewar's Profile" liquor ads; the first series is scheduled to appear in area business magazines. The ads will encourage employers to participate in transportation-related activities by providing a flattering profile of an area employer who has encouraged the use of alternative modes at his/her place of business. After businesses express interest, Metropool will send their account executives to work on-site at employer locations, usually to provide information about different transportation services and to help them develop transportation management plans.

Above: Work/Family Directions, Inc., takes advantage of press coverage to publicize its program.

Below: The Bay Area's Metropolitan Transportation Commission issues a newsletter highlighting its Commuter Check program.

Media advertising has also been used in many urban centers. In Chicago the Regional Transportation Authority promoted its fare voucher program by blanketing the city with radio ads targeted at the non-rider market segment. However, research into the San Francisco Commuter Check program found that high frequency transit riders were far more likely to seek information on the program and to solicit their employer's participation than non-riders or infrequent transit users. While auto drivers are the ultimate target of a subsidy program, the key action that must occur is obtaining employer enrollment, because this is what leads to modal shifts. As auto drivers are less likely to advocate for the program, directly marketing to them has not proven effective in motivating employer enrollment.

Press Conferences and Press Releases

Both press conferences and press releases can be an effective technique for generating broad-based interest in a new program. For example, the TransitChek program staged an introductory press conference in a New York City subway station. The press conference, which included the Mayor and other dignitaries, generated excellent coverage by the local press. The event sparked many inquiries – and subsequent enrollments – from employees seeking to involve their respective companies.

Public Recognition

King County Metro makes a point of publicly recognizing outstanding employers who use their services, thereby publicizing both the services and the businesses that use them. San Francisco's Rides for Bay Area Commuter presented awards to the "100 Best Employees" support traffic reduction efforts. These public recognition ceremonies and awards also give other businesses an incentive to become more involved. Pace has also devised several strategies to recognize participants in its Vanpool Incentive Program and to encourage them to talk about the program with their friends and colleagues. Pace sponsors an annual brunch (complete with a driver-of-the-year award) to thank its vanpool drivers, along with a newsletter for program participants. In addition, the agency has developed a driver longevity program. Five-year drivers receive a sweater, with a discreet embroidered program logo. The incentive choice was carefully considered. Tee shirts and baseball caps were rejected as too casual; Pace chose a sweater to encourage with the expectation that VIP participants would wear them to work and generate interest in the program among fellow employees.

Publications

Working with the press to present stories about new transit products or services can be an effective way to publicize a new program. In addition to working with local newspapers, transit operators can submit articles to organizational newsletters and publications, including chambers of commerce, employer groups, and civic associations. Finally, some transit agencies publish periodic newsletters that provide updates on programs and services.

Chapter 5

Refinement and Reinforcement

Overview

Once a transit-to-business program is implemented, evaluation activities are critical. Program assessment can include both quantitative and qualitative measures of program effectiveness and customer satisfaction. Evaluation activities can range from informal feedback regarding customer satisfaction to sophisticated surveys and indices that measure cost effectiveness and organizational changes.

No matter what technique is used, program evaluation can provide the information necessary to refine and modify marketing programs to maximize their effectiveness. Ideally, evaluation activities should be considered from the start so that the program can incorporate supportive elements. For example, establishing a mailing list and a communications database at first contact allows subsequent marketing evaluation contacts to also be made. Ultimately, the role of marketing evaluation cannot be an afterthought, but a key element in the overall program design and delivery.

Measures of Effectiveness

As discussed in the previous chapter, a detailed communications plan is an essential element of a comprehensive marketing program. One important part of the communications plan would be the envisioned milestones, perhaps stated as measures of success, for all key program elements. This will also help frame efforts to evaluate the effectiveness of the various communications. This may be as simple as tracking the number of responses to various ads, flyers, and other materials, but it can also become more involved. For example, if an advertising effort is found to have created lower response than expected, a more careful evaluation may be needed to ascertain if the message is actually getting to the target decision-makers, or precisely where the strategy is failing. The need to revise the communications plan may be obvious, but exactly how to do may be more elusive. More generally, in any marketing program, directing effort to revealing and incorporating lessons learned in early phases can be critical to success in subsequent phases. Specific approaches to tracking program costs and benefits are discussed below.

> Kaiser Permanente uses three different measures to evaluate the success of a marketing effort:
>
> ❶ Awareness of the organization
> ❷ Number of people who "consider purchasing" the product
> ❸ Change in organizational growth rate

Measuring Costs

Budgets for marketing campaigns are largely dependent on transit agency funding levels, the quantity of service being offered, and the degree to which a completely separate sales staff is employed during the marketing campaign. In established organizations that provide many services and employ a dedicated sales staff, direct marketing costs are much higher than for a small agency where the technical staff is also in charge of marketing and sales. Also, given that many of the smaller agencies do not necessarily have very complicated accounting procedures, it can often be difficult to estimate the level of resources being spent on marketing efforts, especially staff time, as separate from general technical work.

Accounting is not the only obstacle to assessing marketing costs. It appears that most agencies match their marketing efforts to the level of funding they have available, spending as much or as little as their budget allows. RIDES for Bay Area Commuters has had to reduce its marketing budget in recent years due to budget cuts, and this need to adjust to funding levels appears to be a recent characteristic of the ridesharing business. Given this environment, it is difficult to establish a precise measurement of typical marketing costs for most programs. In general, it appears that agencies tend to spend what they can, and hope for the best results at that level of effort.

Measuring Benefits

Few of the transit agencies surveyed for the first phase of this project measured the benefits from a given marketing campaign. This certainly makes it difficult to understand the benefits that have been realized, to separate internal and external influences, or to assess the effects of certain marketing techniques. It was unclear to what extent the agencies surveyed were familiar with the nuances of each of the techniques, and to what extent lack of experience and training may explain the wide variability of the results. (For example, an agency may consider response to a direct mailing disappointing because they do not realize that almost all direct mail campaigns tend to produce low response rates.) For the evaluations that were performed, the quality and depth of analysis varied widely, largely depending on the particular concerns and requirements of the various agencies and their funding sources. This makes it difficult to compare different programs or to draw general conclusions about benefits.

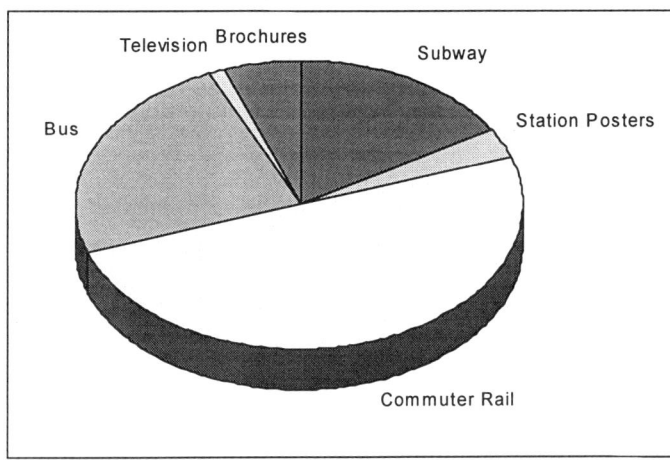

The Philadelphia TransitChek program tracked the effectiveness of different marketing strategies.

Nevertheless, some relatively simple and low-cost strategies are available to transit agencies to track the effectiveness of various marketing programs. For example, the Philadelphia TransitChek program tracked the number of program inquiries from each element of the marketing program. The findings quickly showed the key role that commuter rail passengers played in advancing the voucher program.

Another common strategy is to use one or more measures of cost effectiveness to evaluate the success of a marketing effort. These may include marketing costs per new rider, cost per response to a marketing campaign, or the ratio of marketing costs to revenues. Kaiser Permanente, for example, reviews both internal and external measures to track marketing effectiveness. Kaiser compares the *cost of sales efforts* to the *revenue generated from sales* and measures success by routinely tracking awareness of its name and products, the number of customers who consider enrolling, and various organizational growth rates. Finally, the organization compares its marketing costs to those incurred by other companies, both within the health care industry and elsewhere.

Staff for the New York TransitChek program initially tracked both the number of inquiries and relative cost per inquiry resulting from different communication methods. Yet, staff also sought to examine additional measures of marketing effectiveness, such as the relationship of new enrollments to different marketing techniques. This proved impossible to track, however, because it can take exposure to numerous marketing materials and multiple contacts – sometimes over years – to generate some enrollments. Finally, the staff settled on a year-to-year comparison of total sales to new employers in relation to that year's marketing budget. Measuring *marketing cost per new customer dollar of sales* filters out recurring sales and avoids valuing a new large account the same as a small one, which would happen by tracking only the number of enrollments.

Customer Satisfaction

Many organizations conduct surveys in order to assess customer satisfaction. Bank of America, for example, conducted follow-up research to test the effectiveness of the marketing strategies for the Alpha/Prima Account, while Pace formalized the use of a customer satisfaction monitoring system and a satisfaction index as a route activity and ongoing management tool. A number of transit agencies have developed innovative approaches to gauging customer satisfaction. The Washington Metropolitan Area Transit Authority implemented a "mystery rider" program that uses volunteers to rate their experiences on the Metro system. Use of standardized questionnaires allows tracking over time. Tidewater Regional Transit in Norfolk, Virginia, has a long-standing "bus meisters" program that uses a similar approach. In Los Angeles, the Metropolitan Transportation Authority provides customers with free riders if their bus is more than 15 minutes late. The London Transit Commission, in Ontario, distributed "scratch-off" survey cards three times over a 20-month period to obtain baseline and subsequent data on the impacts of its fare restructuring; the survey was designed to include a number of customer satisfaction inquiries as well. Finally, in Rockland County, New York, the transit operator used a "Commissioner's Hotline" and customer comment cards to solicit rider input for a service improvement program; the agency used interior bus posters and a driver hand-out to promote the program.

> Carefully tracking responses to each newspaper ad it placed, NJ TRANSIT used cost per response to indicate the value of its communications tools. To publicize a major service improvement, the agency sent flyers in a coupon circular to homes in two counties. The response was so strong and the cost so low -- less than one-tenth of what was routinely achieved -- that the agency expanded this marketing approach statewide. This, in turn, led to a major redirection of the marketing plan toward direct mail.

Feedback

Most new products will need some level of refinement and revision over time. Users may need more information than was initially provided, or the benefits that actually appeal to the market may be different from those that were highlighted. More sales support or an enhanced image may be needed. Feedback from clients or customers can help provide transit providers with the information they need to adapt the product or marketing program.

The account executive approach is particularly helpful in this regard. Thanks to the personal relationship that has been forged between the transit agency and the business enterprise, the sales staff can easily stay in touch with client companies, identify any concerns, and find solutions. Agencies can also survey employer contacts about the effectiveness of transit programs or products; these impressions can provide valuable information about the larger number of employees that the contacts represent.

Customer Service Guarantee

The Los Angeles MTA's *On-Time Performance Warranty* provides customers with free rides if their bus is more than 15 minutes late. Other elements of MTA's 1997 Customer Orientation Priority include:

- Customer suggestion forms placed on buses
- Adopt a stop (business involvement opportunity)
- Mystery riders checking on service
- Managers required to occasionally ride buses
- Bus operators receiving too many complaints are assigned to answer the customer service hotline
- Employees who give outstanding customer service receive gifts and bonuses; for example, employees receive a $25 gift certificate for a month without customer complaints
- Held a highly successful Customer First Conference to further develop the culture within the MTA

Without agency support and follow-through on the results of this feedback – modifying the product to better satisfy its market or adjusting the communications plan so that the market expands – long-term success may be limited. Given the large role that customer and business satisfaction plays in determining success with transit-to-business marketing efforts, it is hard to understate the overall importance of the evaluation and follow-through functions.

Chapter 6

Conclusions

Transit to-business marketing offers transit agencies opportunities to add riders and revenue, gain political support, and continue to address mobility, environmental and social issues. It provides a framework for transit to better face its competition and strengthen its market position in both the short- and long-term.

The transit-to-business marketing strategy envisions new markets for transit and improved linkages to existing markets. It reflects a new multi-dimensional or multi-market strategy for transit, and it explicitly acknowledges that transit can influence the demand for its products and services by getting more involved with the actors and forces that create the demand for transit. Transit-to-business marketing is a service development and delivery *process* that integrates support from interested third parties (the business community) to make it easier to gain new riders and ensure their satisfaction with transit.

Thus, transit-to-business marketing is a cooperative process that seeks to meet the interests of employers, retailers, developers and other third parties as a way to better meet the transit agency's own interests. Over time, outreach to the business community also has market-shaping benefits. It can reduce the influence of policies that discourage transit use, like free or heavily subsidized parking, and increase the availability of programs that encourage transit use, like transit benefits, shuttle services, or transit-focused development decisions.

At its core, transit-to-business marketing is a sales function, and a challenging one at that. Partners need to be found and educated about "what's in it for them" in making transit part of their business. As with any sales activity, it is most important that *the customer's wants and needs* be understood. Motivations of both the would-be business partners and the ultimate transit users need to be understood and reflected in the products, programs and services that are delivered. Clearly portraying how the proposed transit-to-business endeavor will serve the goals of the business partners is critical – for financial savings, added customers or sales, improved staff recruitment or retention, added employee morale, or eased parking problems. The benefits of transit-to-business programs are real, and well-prepared brochures, videos, sales presentations and other methods can make these arguments persuasive.

A successful transit-to-business marketing program is also flexible and adaptable, so that it can meet the needs of a wide market or change as necessary over time. Table 6-1 notes some general conclusions that can be offered about the applicability of transit-to-business marketing programs by city size. Yet, the *process* used to develop and implement a transit-to-business marketing program may be as or more important than specific attributes of the selected service, program or product. In its essence, transit- business marketing is a management framework or mind-set. In one of this project's case studies, developing aggressive transit-to-business activities was the primary product of a strategic planning effort that largely redefined the agency. While not every application of transit-to-business marketing efforts need be as all-encompassing as this, this does illustrate the far-reaching implications of this innovative strategy for transit market development.

Table 6-1
Transit-to-Business Program Effectiveness by Area Size

Action	Large City	Medium City	Small City
On-site pass sales	Effective if single operator	Effective	Effective
Pass subsidies	Effective if single operator	Can be effective	Not usually effective
University Passes/EcoPass Program	Effective at large employers/schools if single operator	Can apply at schools and colleges	Can apply at schools and colleges
Vouchers	Very effective, especially with multiple operators	Less effective	Probably not effective
Credit card / third-party billing	Exists in Phoenix only	Could be developed	Probably not effective
Carpooling	Effective	Effective	Effective
Vanpooling	Effective	Can be effective	Probably not effective
Guaranteed ride home	Can be effective in all settings, especially with employer support	Can be effective in all settings, especially with employer support	Can be effective in all settings, especially with employer support
Employee transportation coordinators	Very effective	Less effective	Probably not effective
Transportation management associations	Effective, especially in suburbs	Can be effective	Probably not effective
Shuttle services	Effective, especially in suburbs	Can be effective	Probably not effective
Circulator services	Effective, esp. in suburban areas	Can be effective	Probably not effective
Subscription services	Can be effective	Less effective	Not effective
Reverse commute services	Very effective	Can be effective	Can be effective
Modifying existing services	May not be practical	Very effective	Very effective
Transit enhancements/amenities	Very effective	Very effective	Very effective
Site design initiatives	Very effective	Effective	Effective
Employer survey assistance	Very effective	Very effective	Very effective
Relocation services	Very effective	Can be effective	Can be effective
New employee orientation materials	Very effective	Very effective	Very effective
Transit information services	Effective	Effective	Effective
Retail incentives	Unknown	Effective	May be effective
Media sponsorship	Effective	May be effective	May be effective
Regulatory initiatives	Effective	May be effective	Unknown

Other key lessons revealed from this study are summarized below.

Requirements for Success

Successful transit-to-business marketing programs have a number of elements in common.

- **Understand the Market.** Understanding customers, responding to their needs and selling to them are critical elements of successful transit-to-business marketing activities. Transit agencies can use market research to gain the wisdom to accomplish these tasks.

- **Define the Product.** The more specifically the target market is defined, the easier it is to tailor the product. Research can reveal key design features (e.g., simplicity, flexibility, value, security) or relevant market segments (e.g., large vs. small employers). Customer satisfaction is largely a function of how well a product, and all aspects of its delivery, match the perceived needs of its customers.

- **Sell to the Customer.** The most effective sales approaches are defined by the customer's needs. By responding to customer concerns, the successful sales staff is not selling the product – but selling a solution.

- **Staffing.** Sales positions are not common in public transit agencies, but the sales mentality is a critical function for transit-to-business marketing. It may be the "make it or break it" element determining ultimate success. Staff need to be motivated and recognized for their success.

- **Leadership and Support.** Because they often require organizational change, transit-to-business programs require support from the top levels of a transit agency, as well as agency-wide support at the staff level. Fostering a customer-first mentality is a common element among businesses that seek to regain, retain or notably expand their markets.

Transit-to-Business Marketing Tools

A wide array of communications tools are available to transit agencies pursuing transit-to-business marketing. Specific choices will be determined by the target markets, product elements, and available resources.

- **Direct Sales.** Direct sales techniques are commonly used to make initial contact with potential customers and provide them with information about a product or service. Specific strategies include direct mail, telemarketing and electronic communications media.

- **Personal Selling**. Personal selling includes any direct contact between a transit agency and an employer. Agency staff may include a dedicated sales force, marketing personnel, or technical staff. Contact may include meetings to present product information, on-site events like transportation fairs, or participation in community or civic organizations.

- **Rider-Based Marketing.** Some transit-to-business programs can be marketed by transit riders themselves who can convey the need for a particular service or program to their employers. Employees can deliver program materials to their employer more effectively than any salesperson might, and they can use internal means of advocacy that are not available to outsiders. This method is especially helpful for reaching small employers or when it is hard to justify other sales efforts.

- **Partnerships.** Many transit agencies have developed partnerships with local business and media sponsors to help promote their programs. This approach has proven particularly successful for voucher programs; typically station call letters are printed on program materials in exchange for media time.

- **Advertising and Publicity.** Specific strategies include media advertising, press conferences, newsletters, and other publications.

Program Evaluation

Just as market research is critical to the definition of a successful product, evaluation helps refine and re-direct them. Direct feedback from users can be especially helpful; some describe user feedback as the "golden nuggets" of marketing evaluation. Costs, impacts, satisfaction levels among participants, and reasons for non-involvement by non-participants are primary dimensions for program evaluation activities. Program evaluation should not be an afterthought, but an explicit element in the design of the program or service; few projects hit a bulls-eye on the first shot.

Future Opportunities

Despite rapid growth in recent years, transit-to-business marketing remains an emerging area that is poised to evolve and expand further. Many different types of transit-to-business programs and services exist, and they have different levels of relevance in different transit settings. As transit-to-business linkages can yield relatively immediate pay-offs and potentially far greater long-term impacts, an expanded focus on this area is justified. The area can be addressed incrementally within the focus of existing transit marketing activities, or it might be an important element of new strategic initiatives for addressing some of the basic challenges that transit agencies now face. In either case, further attention to this area could have substantial returns for transit agencies.